SCIENCE SURPRISES™

EVERYDAY PHYSICAL SCIENCE EXPERIMENTS WITH
LIGHT AND SOUND

AMY FRENCH MERRILL

The Rosen Publishing Group's
PowerKids Press™
New York

For Kelli

Some of the experiments in this book are designed for a child to do together with an adult.

Published in 2002 by The Rosen Publishing Group, Inc.
29 East 21st Street, New York, NY 10010

First Edition

Book Design: Michael Caroleo, Michael de Guzman, Nick Sciacca
Project Editor: Frances E. Ruffin

Photo Credits: p. 5 (lightning) © PhotoDisk; p. 5 (drummers) © Kevin R. Morris/CORBIS; all experiment photos by Adriana Skura.

Merrill, Amy French.
Everyday physical science experiments with light and sound / Amy French Merrill.
    p. cm. — (Science surprises)
Includes bibliographical references and index.
  ISBN 0-8239-5804-3 (lib. bdg.)
1. Light—Experiments—Juvenile literature. 2. Sound—Experiments—Juvenile literature. [1. Light—Experiments. 2. Sound—Experiments.
3. Experiments.] I. Title. II. Series.
  QC360 .M47 2002
  535'.078—dc21
                                                                                              2001000256

Manufactured in the United States of America

CONTENTS

BOOM! FLASH! BOOM!

It's a sunny day and the crowd cheers as a marching band parades down the street. Boom! Boom! The drummers pound their drums. Dah-tah-dah! The trumpet players blow their horns. You cover your eyes with your hands as light bounces off the shiny brass instruments. Suddenly the sky grows dark. You see the bright flash of lightning and hear the rumbling sound of thunder. A storm is on its way. The marching band stops playing, and everyone heads for cover.

Sunlight, music, lightning, and thunder all give us important information about the world, through light and sound. How does sunlight reach your eyes? How does music reach your ears? Sound and light move in the same way—they travel in waves.

Sound and light are both forms of energy. ▶

What Is Light?

Light is a form of **energy**. Light comes from many different sources. Some sources of light are natural, such as the Sun and the stars. Other light sources, like lightbulbs and candles, are made by people. If you look at the beam of a flashlight in a dark room, you can see that rays of light travel in straight lines. If you hold an object in front of the flashlight, the rays pass through, bounce off, or are **absorbed** by the

MATERIALS NEEDED:
flashlight, construction paper, pencil, scissors, tape, wooden rod

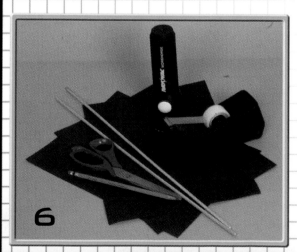

6

object. Take objects that are made of different **materials**, such as a piece of clear glass, a mirror, and a piece of cardboard, and hold them in front of a lit flashlight, one at a time. What do you see? Materials that let light pass through, like glass, are called **transparent**. Materials that stop light from passing through are called **opaque**. When light hits an opaque object, it makes a shadow. To make a fun shadow, draw the outline of an object onto a sheet of construction paper. Cut it out and tape it onto a rod. Facing a blank wall, hold up your cutout in front of a flashlight.

When you keep the light on the cutout but pull the flashlight farther away from it, the shadow ▶ on the wall seems to grow larger.

Reflecting Light

How important is light? Without light you cannot see. You see objects because light bounces, or **reflects**, off them. Different surfaces reflect light in different ways. One way to see with reflected light is through a **periscope**. When a submarine is underwater, a periscope is used to see what's happening on the surface. To make a periscope, cut two **diagonal** slots on opposite sides of a cardboard milk or juice carton. Use a ruler to determine the placement, then draw two lines. Cut the slots. Carefully push a mirror into the top slot so that the mirror side faces down. Push a mirror into the bottom slot so that the mirror side

MATERIALS NEEDED:

milk or juice carton, ruler, pencil, scissors, 2 mirrors, each a bit wider than the carton

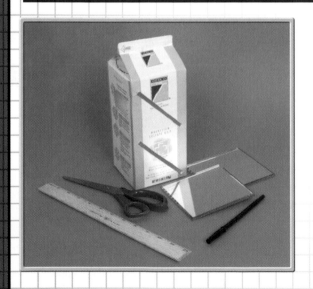

faces up. On the front of the carton, cut out a square opening so that it's facing the top mirror. Punch a hole with a sharpened pencil into the back of the carton near the bottom mirror. Standing near a corner, hold the carton so that only the square looks out from the corner. Peek into the small hole. What do you see? You should be able to see images from around the corner.

Cut slots into the carton carefully so that the mirrors fit and don't slide out.

When light rays enter the square opening, they reflect light from the top mirror onto the bottom mirror. The bottom mirror allows you to see images reflected from the square.

BENDING LIGHT

Light rays change direction when they move from one transparent material to another. For example, light rays bend when they pass from air to water or from water to air. This bending is called **refraction**.

MATERIALS NEEDED:

glass of water, spoon

Here's an experiment to try. Rest a spoon at an angle in a glass of water. Stand back and look at the glass. The spoon appears to bend into two sections. Why does the spoon look bent? This is because the light rays bend as they pass from water into air. The bending light rays make the spoon look as though it is bending, too.

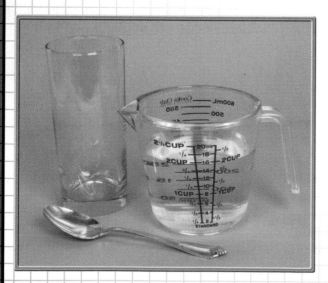

What makes the spoon look as though it is bent? ▶

Refraction is a property of light that is very useful. Lenses are curved pieces of glass that refract light in a certain way to correct a person's vision. Lenses are used in eyeglasses, magnifying glasses, microscopes, and telescopes.

◀ Rest a spoon at an angle in a glass of water.

THE COLOR OF LIGHT

What color is light? It is all colors! Sunlight may appear colorless, but it really is a mixture of several different colors. You can see some of these colors when a rainbow appears in the sky after a storm. A rainbow forms when light from the Sun is refracted, or bent, as it passes through raindrops in the air. You also can see a rainbow when you place a **prism** on a sheet of white paper and shine a light through it.

Here's an experiment that shows that light is a mixture of colors. Cut a circle from a piece of white cardboard. Divide the circle evenly

MATERIALS NEEDED:

white cardboard, scissors, ruler, paints or markers (red, orange, yellow, green, blue, indigo, violet), paintbrushes (if paint is used), toothpick

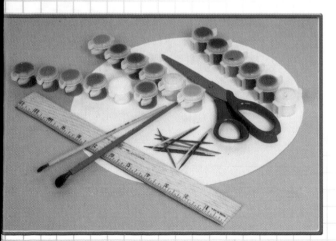

into seven sections. Paint each section with one of the colors of the **spectrum**: red, orange, yellow, green, blue, indigo, and violet. Make a tiny hole in the center of the circle and fit a toothpick into it. Spin the wheel. What happens to the colors?

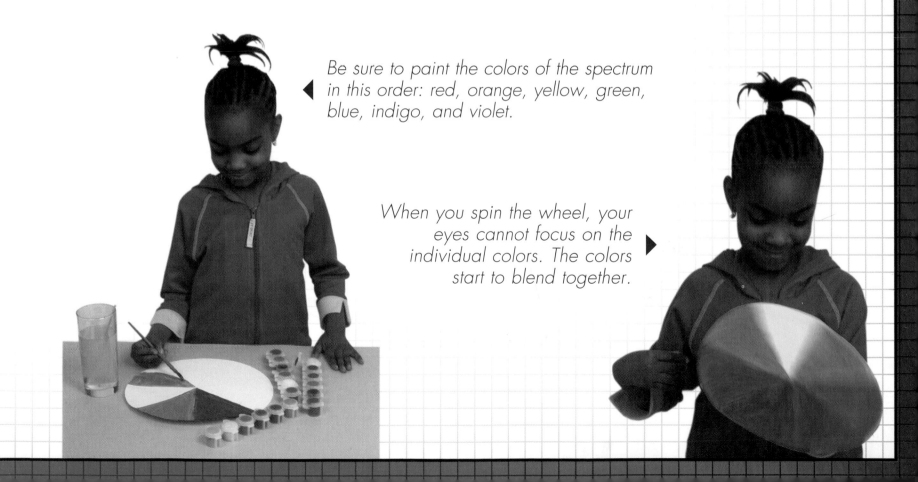

◀ *Be sure to paint the colors of the spectrum in this order: red, orange, yellow, green, blue, indigo, and violet.*

When you spin the wheel, your eyes cannot focus on the individual colors. The colors start to blend together. ▶

What Is Sound?

Sounds are caused by **vibrations**. When an object vibrates, it moves the air around it. You can hear and can feel vibrations. You can't see vibrations in the air, but you can see and can hear the things they affect, like a drum or a piano.

Try this experiment. Stretch a sheet of plastic wrap tightly over a large, round container, such as a cake pan or a large, plastic bowl. Use a large rubber band to hold the plastic in place. You've made a drum. Then sprinkle a spoonful of rice on top of the plastic. Hold a flat, metal pan slightly above your "drum" and tap the flat, metal pan with a wooden spoon or a ruler.

> **MATERIALS NEEDED:**
> round container, such as a cake pan or plastic bowl; flat, metal pan; plastic wrap; large rubber band; rice; wooden spoon or ruler

When you tap the pan, the metal vibrates. The vibrations move the air around the tray. When these vibrations reach the plastic, the plastic vibrates, too.
When this happens, the rice moves!

You hear sounds when vibrations reach your ear. ▶

Sound Waves

Sound travels in waves. When an object vibrates, **molecules** in the air are squeezed together and then are stretched apart. This squeezing and stretching of air molecules makes the sound you hear.

Sound waves travel through the air in all directions. Here's a way to **model** sound waves. Fill a container with water. Larger containers, like a sink, tub, or plastic dishpan, work better. Add a few drops of food coloring. Drop a pebble into the water. What do you see? Ring-shaped waves travel out in all directions. Try dropping two pebbles in the water at the same time but in different places. Two

MATERIALS NEEDED:
large bowl, water, food coloring, pebbles

pebbles make two sets of waves that pass through each other. Sound waves move in a similar way. That's why you can hear several different kinds of sound at one time.

Drop a pebble in water and ring-shaped waves will move out in all directions. ▶

◀ *When sound is made, sound waves cause tiny hairs in our inner ears to vibrate. These hairs help us to hear sound.*

How Sound Travels

Sound waves travel not only through air, which is a gas, but also through solids and liquids. In fact sounds travel faster in solids and liquids than they do in either gases or air. You can hear this for yourself. To hear sound travel through a solid, place a book on a table. Lay one ear on the book and use your hand to cover your other ear. Ask a friend to tap on the table next to the book. How does the tapping sound? Fill a plastic bag with water and seal it. Place the bag on a table, and lay your ear on the bag. How does the tapping sound now? Blow air into a plastic bag and seal it. Now listen to the

MATERIALS NEEDED:

table, book, plastic bag filled with water, plastic bag filled with air

◀ *What other kinds of solid materials might give you a different sound?*

tapping a third time. What happened? Molecules are closer together in solids than in liquids and closer together in liquids than in gases. Sound waves travel from molecule to molecule. The closer together the molecules are, the faster and better the sound waves travel. There are no sounds in outer space. Outer space is a **vacuum**, which is a space with no air or other matter. Objects may be able to vibrate, but no sounds are heard. Without air molecules, sound can't travel to our ears.

Imagine listening to sound under water. ▶

THE SOUNDS OF MUSIC

Musical instruments produce beautiful sounds. There are many kinds of musical instruments, and the sounds produced by each kind are different, too.

Although they do it in different ways, all musical instruments create sounds through vibrations. The different sounds of a wind instrument, like a flute or a pipe organ, come from vibrations of air blown through a column. When the column of air in the instrument is shorter, a high sound is produced. When the column is longer, a low sound is made.

Try making your own pipe organ. Cut eight drinking straws into eight

MATERIALS NEEDED:
8 plastic drinking straws, scissors, tape

different lengths. Cut one end of each straw into a point. Line up the straws from long to short. Secure the set of eight straws across the middle the set of straws with tape on both sides. Hold your pipe organ about ½ inch (1.3 cm) from your mouth and blow. How does a straw's length affect the sound it makes?

▲

Pipe organs played by early humans were made from reeds, the stems of grasses that grew in swamps.

Try making a pipe organ with only 6 straws and one with 10 straws. How different is the sound? ▶

So Much Sound, So Much Light

How do people use sound and light? We use both to communicate, educate, warn, and entertain for starters. Have you ever heard the phrase "A picture is worth a thousand words"? Photographs—pictures created with light—are lasting images of people, places, and events in history. Traffic lights help to direct cars, trucks, and buses. Powerful beams of light, called lasers, read special codes of information on items at the supermarket.

Animals such as bats and dolphins use echoes from the high sounds they make to help them find their way. Scientists use **sonar** equipment on ships and submarines in much the same way. Musicians compose and perform beautiful music. Fireworks explode in brilliant displays of sound and light. Television programs and movies depend on sound and light, too. How do people use sound and light? We use them every day, in every way!

GLOSSARY

absorbed (uhb-ZORBD) To take in moisture, heat, and light.

diagonal (dy-AG-ih-nul) A straight line that cuts across in slanting directions.

energy (EH-nur-jee) The power to work or act. Light, heat, and electricity are among different forms of energy.

materials (muh-TEER-ee-uhlz) What things are made from or used for.

model (MAH-dil) A representation of something that later will be made.

molecules (MAH-lih-kyoolz) Tiny building blocks that make up a substance.

opaque (oh-PAYK) When something is so thick that light cannot pass through it.

periscope (PEHR-ih-skohp) A tool that sticks out from the top of a submarine and is used to see ships, land, and other things above the surface of the water.

prism (PRIH-zum) A triangular block of glass that separates white light into the seven colors of the rainbow.

reflects (rih-FLEKTS) Throws back light, heat, or sound.

refraction (rih-FRAK-shun) Bending something, such as a light ray or sound wave.

sonar (SOH-nar) A system using reflected underwater sound waves to detect and locate objects or distances.

spectrum (SPEC-trum) The colors that make up a rainbow.

transparent (trans-PAYR-ent) Something that allows light through so that things can be seen on the other side.

vacuum (VA-kyoom) A space that is empty of air and all matter.

vibrations (vy-BRAY-shunz) Rapid movement back and forth.

INDEX

WEB SITES

To learn more about light and sound, check out this Web site:
http://library.thinkquest.org/11924/